LRRP's in action

By John Burford

Color by Don Greer

Illustrated by Joe Sewell

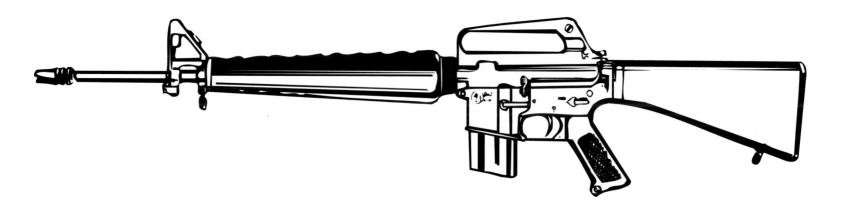

G000150194

Combat Troops Number 11
squadron/signal publications

SGT Thomas Brooks moves up a stream in search of a place to climb up the steep banks. He is carrying an M-16 rifle with an experimental sound suppressor.

ISBN 0-89747-312-2

If you have any photographs of aircraft, armor, soldiers or ships of any nation, particularly wartime snapshots, why not share them with us and help make Squadron/Signal's books all the more interesting and complete in the future. Any photograph sent to us will be copied and the original returned. The donor will be fully credited for any photos used. Please send them to:

Squadron/Signal Publications, Inc.
1115 Crowley Drive.
Carrollton, TX 75011-5010

Acknowledgements:

U.S. Army   Ron Kiser
John Looney   Jim Mesko

Dedication:

To General William C. Westmoreland, founder of the RECONDO School.

A 25th Infantry Division LRRP team works on patrol movement training near the Cu Chi base camp. When a team wasn't out on a mission, their spare time was spent in training to sharpen their skills. Such training might actually save a life in the field, when decisions had to be made in split seconds. (Author)

3

Introduction

The American Civil War saw the introduction of a new type of land warfare which made wide spread use of fortified defensive lines or trenches. This new form of land warfare gave birth to the static Front Line and a loss of mobility. It also created a glaring need for the commanders of both warring sides to see behind those lines and learn what moves their opponent was preparing for. In the American Civil War the observation balloon was one of the first technical ways for commanders to "see behind the lines." Another way to see behind the lines was not technical in nature, but rather used a quick hit and run reconnaissance by a small unit

Major H. A. Williams was the director of the Alamo Scout Training Center during the Second World War. Major Williams was instrumental in the development of the training cycle for the school and in the selection of the men for the training. He took command when the school was officially formed on 12 August 1944. This school was the forerunner of all LRRP training in the U. S. Army. (U. S. Army)

of cavalry. Neither attempt was met with great battlefield success, and the commanders of both armies fought their battles in the blind most of the time, lacking any real time intelligence of the enemy's intentions or dispositions.

The First World War was another war of great trenches and once again new ways of gathering military intelligence were needed. The observation balloon was once again called to action, and a new tool of war, the airplane, was used to gather information on the enemies rear area. The commanders needed to know what was going on in the rear areas of their enemies so they could counter a move by the opposition and effectively direct artillery fire against enemy buildups. The infantry of the various combatants formed small units to infiltrate the enemy trench lines and gather information on the enemy. These actions; however, were of limited success and did not penetrate deep enough behind the lines to get all of the needed information. At the end of the First World War there still wasn't a fast, sure way to gather behind the lines information. The blinders were still on the commanders of the world's armies.

At the dawn of the Second World War the airplane had under gone a number of refinements, and was to become a major tool for collecting enemy information from behind the lines. Two other new tools of modern warfare had also been perfected. These new tools, the radio and the motorized unit, had been developed, refined, and joined together. This combination gave the army commander a new type of unit that could operate deep in the enemy rear area and quickly report information on any enemy movements. The British made a major jump forward in the field of behind the lines reconnaissance with the development of several different elite reconnaissance units. Three of the more recognized of these units were the Long Range Penetration Group of Burma, the Long Range Desert Group of North Africa, and the Special Air Service. Of these, the Special Air Service is still in existence today.

The American Army in the Second World War was a little slow on seeing the need for special reconnaissance units. In late 1943, however, there was one long range reconnaissance unit formed in the South Pacific Theater of Operations. This unit, the Alamo Scouts, was the only true effort by American forces to develop and use long range reconnaissance patrols during the entire war. The Alamo Scouts operated on foot and either walked through the enemy lines, parachuted in, or infiltrated in from the sea to accomplish their missions.

The Korean War saw the American Army once more depending on reconnaissance and spotter aircraft for their behind the lines reconnaissance. The lessons learned from the Alamo Scouts of the Second World War were forgotten. There were some behind the lines combat patrols made by the Ranger Companies in Korea; before they were broken up and assigned to the various Infantry divisions fighting in the war zone, but there weren't any true long range patrol units active in the U. S. Army during the Korean war.

The Cold War that developed after the Second World War saw the North Atlantic Treaty Organization (NATO) allies rethink the need for behind the lines intelligence and reconnaissance. There had been a number of advances made in reconnaissance technology during the late 1950s, as well as a number of advances in countermeasures. The NATO battle plan called for strong defense to grind down the first echelon attacking troops, with air strikes and the new short range artillery missiles to interdict the second echelon attack troops, along with the third echelon supply units. For this strategy to work properly the commanders needed real time information on the location, type, and direction of movement of the targets. The British, Belgian, Dutch and German forces all developed the Long Range Reconnaissance Patrol Company as their answer to this problem, and attached one to each of their operational Corp in the European Theater. Once more the American Commanders were slow to act, but the

The Alamo Scout Training Center was located on Ferguson Island near Dutch New Guinea in the South Pacific and began operations during mid-January of 1944. The men passing under the sign are heading for the machine gun range for training on the Thompson .45 caliber submachine gun, which was the weapon of choice for an Alamo Scout. (U. S. Army)

Students of the Alamo Scouts school are paired off to go through hand-to-hand combat training. Hand-to-hand combat was just one of the many ways the Alamo Scouts were taught to survive and to kill silently while on a mission behind enemy lines. (U. S. Army)

LRRP concept did finally take hold. During 1961, the U. S. Army formed two Long Range Reconnaissance Patrol companies and attached them to their V and VII Army Corps stationed in West Germany.

The war in Vietnam lacked a front line but the enemies strategy made LRRPs a needed tool. The ground commanders who fought the day to day war saw the need for special reconnaissance units at the onset of the fighting during 1965 and formed provisional LRRP units from any assets they could spare. General Westmoreland also understood this need and helped formalize an arrangement between Special Forces and the regular army units to train the men who made up these units. During late 1967, the Army Chief of Staff recognized the need to formalize LRRP units in Vietnam and the orders were cut to create LRRP companies for all of the Division size units and Detachments were created for the separate Army Light Brigades. The gadget makers still tried to replace men with technology and many devices were rained down on the jungle in an effort to find the shadowy enemy, but the human factor could not be replaced. Not being able to leave a good thing alone, the Army decided to convert all LRRP companies to Ranger companies in 1969. The birth of the lettered 75th Ranger companies saw the slow death of the pure long range reconnaissance patrol unit and the start of the long range patrol unit which was a more direct action unit.

The end of the war in Vietnam saw the end of American long range reconnaissance efforts. The lettered 75th Ranger companies were disbanded from the active Army. There were a few National Guard LRRP companies left intact to support the Army Corp in Europe and all else was swept away. Our NATO allies kept their LRRP units and built them up to gain a strong human element in reconnaissance and intelligence gathering. The U. S. Army turned to the gadget makers and tried once again to get technology to do it all. From 1972 until 1986, the U. S. Army toyed around with gadget and counter-gadget, but in the end they realized they could not replace the good old human eyeball with all of their exotic gadgets.

The LRSUs were created in 1986, and each Division and Corp was assigned a detachment. The acronym LRSU stands for Long Range Surveillance Unit, and that is their mission. LRSUs should not be confused with Special Forces or the Ranger Regiments. While the LRSU must be trained as well or better than Special Forces or the men of the Ranger

Regiments, they do not have any direct action requirement. The LRSU is a pure reconnaissance tool and was treated as such. The U. S. Army has assigned all of the LRSU units to the divisions Intelligence Battalion. The American army has finally started to catch up with its European Allies in the field of reconnaissance and intelligence gathering that is focused on the human element. 1990 saw the LRSUs come into their own as they pulled mission after mission during Operation DESERT SHIELD and Operation DESERT STORM.

The Alamo Scouts

The lineage and heraldry of the modern Long Range Reconnaissance Patrol (LRRP) and Long Range Surveillance Unit (LRSU) soldiers is traced through the U. S. Army Special Forces and the 75th Rangers, but the roots of the American Long Range Patrol concept can be traced directly back to the Second World War. These roots go back to the U. S. Sixth Army in the Pacific theater of operation and to a small but outstanding group of men known as — Alamo Scouts.

Upon assuming command of the Sixth Army in February of 1943 Lieutenant General Walter Krueger faced numerous challenges. High on his priority list was the effort to solve the problem of the lack of reliable intelligence. He needed a method to obtain accurate information on the enemy all across the Sixth Armies area of operation. During November of 1943, General Krueger created a training center for select volunteers to be trained in reconnaissance and

Major General J. P. Swift, Commanding General of the 1st Cavalry Division, looks on while Lieutenant Rowland fires a Thompson submachine gun into the water near where trainees are swimming. The idea was to train the men to duck under the water to dodge the bullets and hide from enemy gunners if fired on by the enemy during a water crossing. (U. S. Army)

raider work. General Krueger, a true Texan, selected a name for this group from the name of his Sixth Army Headquarters — The Alamo Force.

Colonel Horton White was given overall responsibility for the creation, training, and employment of the Alamo Scouts. He established the Alamo Scout School on Ferguson Island, near Dutch New Guinea. Colonel White picked Colonel Frederick Bradshaw to be in charge of day-to-day operations of the training center. Colonel Bradshaw personally selected each soldier that attended the training center. The men were selected on the basis of having the highest level of courage, stamina, intelligence and ability to adapt to changing conditions in the field. Any man could be accepted into training regardless of his military experience or his current military occupation specialty.

The Alamo Scout School was commanded by Major H. A. Williams and the training cycle lasted four weeks. The training was rugged, real and demanding. Hours were spent in hand-to-hand combat training as well as physical exercise training. Map reading and jungle survival were stressed, as well as intense weapons training. During one part of the training the men would swim out from shore while a school cadre would fire a Thompson sub-machine gun into the water so the men would learn to duck beneath the water to dodge the bullets and hide from the enemy gunner. Another training exercise would have the men jump into the water with their weapon and all of their equipment and swim to the far shore. There was a special enemy headquarters set up in an abandoned village, and it was used to train the men in assault and raider tactics. The men were trained to perform static surveillance, deep reconnaissance and limited combat operations.

The school graduated ten classes with an average of thirty men per class. The cream of the school graduates formed the ten Alamo Scout teams that were created. Each team consisted

Major General F.H. Osborn talks with Private First Class Raupa about this phase of Alamo Scout training. The men have just finished an exercise that required them to jump in the water with full equipment and weapon and swim to the far shore. The scouts are armed with what appears to be Springfield rifles for training. They would be issued either Thompsons or M-2 carbines for combat operations. (U. S. Army)

of one officer and six enlisted men. The balance of the school graduates would return to their units to form Intelligence and Reconnaissance Platoons for their Regimental Headquarters.

Virtually every major operation of the Sixth Army during the period January of 1944 to April of 1945 was preceded by Alamo Scout surveillance or deep reconnaissance of enemy units and installations in the upcoming area of operations. The Alamo Scouts were not just limited to reconnaissance work. The Scouts were the reconnaissance element for a hostage rescue operation staged by Colonel Mucci's 6th Ranger Battalion. This operation rescued some 512 survivors of the Bataan Death March from a Japanese prison camp.

The Alamo Scouts also conducted a second P0W rescue operation by themselves. The Alamo Scouts proved that good training and a hand picked selection of men were the key to combat success for small units. A shining tribute to the Alamo Scouts was the fact that they were involved in over eighty missions in an extremely hostile environment, and not one man was killed or captured.

The Alamo Scouts performed some direct action but their main mission was static surveillance and deep reconnaissance. The way they were picked, the way they were trained, and their primary mission forge the links between the Alamo Scouts and the Long Range Reconnaissance Patrols and Long Range Surveillance Units that followed them in later wars.

PFC Boes charges into the mock Jap Headquarters that was set up in an abandoned village near the training compound with his weapon blazing. The smoke in front of him came from the hand grenade he threw before starting the assault. He is armed with a .45 caliber Thompson submachine gun. (U. S. Army)

Lieutenant General Walter Krueger, founding father of the Alamo Scouts and commanding General of the Sixth Army, inspects a class at the Scout School during August of 1944. (U. S. Army)

CPL McDonald makes his run on the mock Japanese Headquarters building. The training was made as real as possible to condition the men for the missions ahead. All exercises were live fire with real ammunition and there was no room for error. (U. S. Army)

7

Two Alamo Scout teams at their base camp which was located near the 6th Army Headquarters at Dregor Harbor, Finchhafen, New Guinea during 1944. The men carry a mix of weapons including Thompson submachine guns, M-1/2 carbines and M-1 Grand rifles. (U. S. Army)

There was no shortage of bravery in the Alamo Scouts. Private First Class A.L. Hall and Private L. Belson are awarded the Silver Star medal for bravery in combat from Major Williams, commanding officer of the Alamo Scout School, on 22 June 1944. (U. S. Army)

(Left) The Intelligence and Reconnaisance Platoon of the 126th Infantry Regiment. These men were graduates of the Alamo Scout School who were returned to their units to form their own partols to collect information for the regimental commanders. This group is leaving for a mission into enemy territory on 17 January 1944. The team leader is Lieutenant Murry. the other members are SSGT Young, PFC Haugas, PVT Stockman, PVT Stewart, PVT Tinder, PFC Bellikka, SGT Vladick, PVT Wagner and PVT Wheaton. (U. S. Army)

Rations carried by the Alamo Scouts consisted of standard Army K rations. One days rations included: breakfast; coffee, ham and eggs, fig bar, biscuits, cigarette and chewing gum. Supper was candy bar, stick of gum, package of bouillon powder, four cigarettes, one can of pork luncheon meat and two packs of biscuits. Dinner rations were the same as the supper ration. (U. S. Army)

Alamo Scout Weapons

Thompson .45 Caliber
Submachine Gun

M-1/2 Carbines

Colonel H. V. White presenting the diplomas to the men of the graduating class from the Alamo Scout School on 9 September 1944. (U. S. Army)

Major General Innis Swift, Commanding General of the lst Corp inspecting the 28 October 1944 graduating class. Many members of the class would return to their respective units to form special reconnaissance units within those units. The success of the scouts generated a great deal of interest in the school from all of the top brass. (U. S. Army)

Early LRRPs

As the Cold War began to heat up during the late 1950s and Army units were deployed to Europe, especially West Germany, the Army started to rethink the need for Long Range Reconnaissance Patrol (LRRP) companies. This new thinking was inspired by the British Special Air Service (SAS) idea of small independently operating reconnaissance teams, and the general North Atlantic Treaty Organization (NATO) Air-Land Battle plan. The NATO battle plan called for the ground forces to fight a vigorous forward defense in the border battle area at the start of hostilities and then perform a gradual fighting withdrawal to newly prepared defense positions to grind down and bloody the attacking forces. NATO air forces were assigned to gain control of the airspace over the battle area. When the air superiority is established the air forces were to carry out air-to-ground attacks against the second echelon attack troops coming forward to reinforce point attack units, and fly further back to perform interdiction attacks against the third echelon supply units coming up from the rear areas. The ground forces were to be reinforced by fresh units flown in from Canada and the United States.

The mission given to the LRRP units was to conduct passive deep penetration up to 150 kilometers behind the advancing enemy forces and set up an intelligence collection system for the Army Corps operating in the defense. The patrols were to be infiltrated through enemy lines by air, ground, water or by conducting stay behind operations. By staying behind, the team has the best chance of staying undetected by the forces that overrun their position and are in the best area to be effective in their information gathering role. Once in place, the patrol would establish a well concealed observation post to keep the enemy supply/advance routes under surveillance and report the movement of enemy forces in real time to the Corp Commander. The teams were also tasked to perform point and area reconnaissance as directed by higher headquarters. The role of the LRRP team was passive intelligence collection. LRRP teams were not tasked or designed for direct action missions. The men must undertake

extreme measures to remain undetected by enemy forces or local civilians during their mission.

The intelligence gathered by the team is reported back using Morse code with a TRC-77 AM single-sideband radio using a burst transmission device. The burst transmission device will transmit a 12 to 15 word per minute Morse code message in a matter of seconds and protects the team from detection by radio direction finders. The message was routed to a receiver in friendly territory and then forwarded to the Corp headquarters where the information was used to plan movement or direct air and artillery strikes on the enemy rear area.

The first U. S. Army LRRP units were small test teams formed during 1958 to explore the LRRP concept. The test units worked out well and the U. S. Army decided to develop two companies. On 15 July 1961, the first two official Long Range Reconnaissance Patrol Companies were activated in West Germany. The units were attached to the U. S. Seventh Army. The 3779th LRRP company was assigned to the V Corp at Wildflecken Training area and the 3780th LRRP company was assigned to the VII Corp at Nellingen Training area. The companies were commanded by a major and consisted of a headquarters platoon, two patrol platoons with eight four man patrols in each platoon, a communications platoon, and a transportation platoon. Volunteers were recruited from the Seventh Army with the bulk of the men coming from the 504th and 505th Airborne Battle Groups assigned to the 8th Infantry Division

In May of 1965, the 3779th was changed to Company D (Long Range Reconnaissancce Patrol - LRRP) 17th Infantry and the 3780th was converted to Company C (LRRP) 58th Infantry. Both units were still assigned to the V and VII Corps of the Seventh Army. The companies were moved to the Continental United States during 1968 as part of a U. S. and Soviet forces reduction agreement for Germany. Company D (LRRP) 17th Infantry went to Fort Benning, Georgia and Company C (LRRP) 58th Infantry ended up in Fort Carson,

The unit insignia was painted on the company sign of the the 3779th Long Range Reconnaissance Patrol company in the Wildflecken Training Area, West Germany. This unit was classified as an airborne unit under the U.S. 7th Army. (Ron Kiser)

A group from the 3779th LRRP Company prepare to make a practice parachute jump from an Army H-34 helicopter. At this time making parachute jumps from helicoters was very new and no one had a great deal of experience. (Ron Kiser)

Leroy Roy and Ron Kiser take a rest break and warm up by a campfire in the Fulda Training Area after training maneuvers. Both men are armed with 7.62MM M-14 rifles which can be seen leaning up against the trees. In addition, both men carried standard Army ruck sacks. (Ron Kiser)

7.62MM NATO M-14A-1 Rifle

Some men of Company D (Long Range Reconnaissance Patrol -- LRRP) 17th Infantry, attached to the V Corp, working with explosives at the demolition training pit during 1965. After being withdrawn from Germany, Company D was transferred to Fort Benning, Georgia. (Ron Kiser)

A check point on the Czechoslovakian border near the Fulda Gap. The Fulda Gap was the natural attack route from Eastern Europe into the middle of West Germany. It was part of the operational area assigned to units of V Corps and the ideal place to leave behind a team in the event of an attack. (Ron Kiser)

11

Team members from the V Corps LRRP company transportation section work on the companies radio trucks. These trucks would be used as radio relays for teams in the field. (Ron Kiser)

Colorado. The two units were still attached to the Seventh Army and would deploy to Germany in the event of hostilities.

The Army National Guard formed its first two LRRP companies during 1967 when Company D and Company E (LRRP) 151st Infantry were activated in Indiana. In 1968, the Michigan Army National Guard followed up with the activation of Company E and Company F (LRP) 425th Infantry. Company D (LRRP) 151st Infantry was the only Reserve component infantry unit to serve in Vietnam. They deployed in-country from December of 1968 until December of 1969.

The 7.62MM NATO Standard M-14A1 Rifle was the standard weapon issued to the team members when the companies were formed in 1961. The 5.56MM M-16A1 was issued to the units during 1965 when all U. S. Army Airborne units were given the weapon. The teams had to carry the regular issue Combat Meal Individual (CMI) which weighed over 22 ounces and were bulky to carry. There were no special camouflage uniforms issued by the Army in Europe during this period so the men had to make do with the regular issue uniforms. There were sterile uniforms in stock for the men to use in case of war, and each company had a supply of Warsaw Pact and NATO individual weapons.

The LRRP companies trained for insertion by night parachute drop most of the time, and they did a lot of river crossing exercises when they trained for the stay behind insertion. The average field exercise consisted of a five day mission that ended with the team using E & E (Escape and Evasion) as their method of extraction. The men of these companies were well trained in map reading, enemy vehicle identification, Morse code, and hand-to-hand combat.

A team of LRRPs line up to board a C-130 transport for a training jump into the Fulda training area, West Germany, at the start of a Field Training Exercise (FTX). Parachuting was one method of inserting a team behind enemy lines. (Ron Kiser)

The 3779th LRRP Company changed its insignia and sign when they moved to a new base location near Frankfort Main, West Germany. The insignia consisted of Yellow parachute and wings, a Red lightning bolt, Black V outlined in Gray and the logo airborne in Black. (Ron Kiser)

LRRPs in Vietnam 1965-1967

As the U. S. Army entered the war in Vietnam during May of 1965 it found itself involved in a type of combat for which it was ill-suited and untrained. There had been very little training given to the combat units in unconventional warfare, and very little thought had been given to the problem of finding an elusive enemy in the natural concealment provided by the jungles of Vietnam. During the same time period the U. S. Army in Europe had Long Range Reconnaissance Patrols at the Corp level, but the idea was not carried over to the Army Corps in Vietnam.

The Special Forces in Vietnam had created special LRRP Detachments during 1964 when they activated Detachments B-52, B-50 and B-56. Project Delta, Detachment B-52, was one of the most highly decorated units of its size during the entire war in Vietnam, and it was this unit that General Westmoreland turned to when the need arose to train the fledgling provisional Long Range Reconnaissance Patrol (LRRP) units created by the Army Brigades and Divisions in the field.

General Westmoreland had always been the champion of the small, well trained patrol, and he had created the RECONDO school at Fort Campbell, Kentucky in 1958. General Westmoreland commanded the 101st Airborne Division at that time and the school was designed to teach the divisions E-4s and E-5s in the techniques of patrolling and small unit leadership. It was considered a mini-Ranger school and had its own distinctive pocket patch that was worn by all of the school's graduates while they were assigned to the 101st Division. This pocket patch, a White arrowhead with 101 across it, was used as a hat patch on the Black baseball caps worn by the men of Company F, 58th LRRP, 101st Airborne during 1968. The RECONDO patch was also used by the Reconnaissance platoons in the 1st Brigade before Company F was formed.

Members of the Long Range Reconnaissance Patrol unit of the 1st Brigade, 101st Airborne Division listen to a briefing from the brigade commander, Brigadier General Willard Pearson. The briefing was for Operation Eagle Bait that was to run during July of 1966 near the division base camp at Phan Rang. (U.S. Army)

Members of the 196th Light Infantry Brigade LRRP unit take a break before leaving to patrol an area fifteen miles northwest of Tay Ninh during March of 1967. The Tiger Stripe uniform was the favorite uniform for LRRPs until the random leaf pattern camouflage uniform was made the standard field uniform during 1968. (U.S. Army)

13

Two members of the Reconnaissance Platoon 2\502, lst Brigade, 101st Airborne Division bring in captured horses to be airlifted back to the Division rear area during August of 1966. During late 1967, the Army would recruit men from the different division Recon Platoons to fill the slots for the newly formed LRRP Companies that were to be activated in January of 1968. (U.S. Army)

With General Westmoreland's blessing the provisional LRRP units were created, trained and equipped. Both the training and the equipment came from the 5th Special Forces Group which had its headquarters at Nha Trang Republic of Vietnam (RVN). The famous Tiger Stripe uniform was bought commercially by the Special Forces for the use of its indigenous troops and many American troops wedged themselves into the Asian Large Tiger Stripe uniform issued to them between 1965 and 1967. Other favorite items were the indigenous rucksack and poncho, both of these items were small, light, tough and fit in with the mission much better than the larger and heavier American equipment.

On 15 September 1966, the Military Advisery Command Vietnam-RECONDO school was made official under the title MACV-RECONDO. Before that time, the school's instructors were part of the Delta project and were not assigned to full time training duty at the RECONDO school. The Army in Vietnam was waking up to the fact that it needed Long Range Reconnaissance Patrol Companies for each Division and Detachments for each Brigade, and the wheels were set in motion to activate these units.

The provisional LRRP units that were formed in late 1965 laid the ground-work for all future Long Range Reconnaissance Patrol missions run during the war. The different unit

Two LRRPs of the 25th Infantry Division being extracted from the dense jungle north of Cu Chi by a McGuire rig during 1967. When the extraction helicopter could not land, the McGuire rig was the only other option. While it looks exciting, most LRRPs reported that they really did not enjoy the flight home dangling under the Huey. (U. S. Army)

Members of a LRRP unit from the 25th Infantry Division race for cover after being insurted into enemy territory by a UH-1 Huey helicopter. The insurtion was the most dangerous time for the LRRP team, and these men have cleared the helicopter before it landed. This mission was a partol north of CuChi during January of 1967. Both men are armed with light weight Colt 5.56MM M-16 rifles. (U. S. Army)

Colt 5.56MM M-16 Rifle

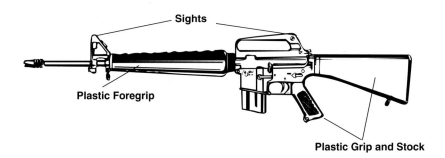

Sights

Plastic Foregrip

Plastic Grip and Stock

General Person talks with the men on the provisional LRRP Platoon attached to the 1st Brigade, 101st Airborne Division. General Person expanded the use of long range reconnaissance patrols by the brigade. The Tiger Stripe uniforms were obtained from the 5th Special Forces Group. (Ken Miller)

commanders manipulated personnel assignments and took volunteers to form their LRRP units. Many of the early LRRP troops were technically assigned to the various Brigades anti-tank platoons, which weren't used in Vietnam.

One of the first uses of LRRPs by the 101st Airborne came during Operation CHECKERBOARD in December of 1965. While the 2\327 assumed the area defense of the Phan Rang base camp, the LRRPs were used to conduct patrols outside the Phan Rang area to insure the enemy didn't move a force into a position to attack the base camp. The extra effort was made so the rest of the Brigade could come to Phan Rang and all the men in the Brigade could enjoy a quiet and secure Christmas day. The teams consisted of six men; a team leader, forward observer, radio operator, and three riflemen. Later, in 1966, the team structure was altered to

A LRRP team leader of LRRP Unit D, 1st Squadron, 4th Cavalry, 1st Infantry Division signals his men while on patrol during 1967. Hand signals allowed for silent communications. The area being patrolled consisted of rice paddies in the III Corps area, the openness of the rice paddys made it very difficult to remain concealed. The team leader is armed with a CAR-15, the carbine variant of the M-16 5.56MM rifle. (U.S. Army)

add an extra radio man. The new structure was team leader, assistant team leader, senior radio operator, second radio operator, senior scout and second scout. This new structure insured that a team could still function even if took casualties while on a mission.

In January of 1966, General Willard Pearson took command of the 1st Brigade, 101st Airborne and the units of the Brigade intensified their combat activity. February of 1966 saw the Brigade move northwest of Tuy Hoa to find the North Vietnam Army's (NVA) 95th Regiment. This action was titled Operation HARRISON. Among the innovations used by General Pearson during this operation was the expanded use of long range reconnaissance patrols to assist the Brigade in finding the elusive enemy. April of 1966 saw the lst Brigade move to Phan Thiet to conduct operations with South Vietnamese (ARVN) forces. This was the first presence of a major foreign military unit in this area since 1954 when two French Regiments were destroyed in that area by Viet Minh Communist forces. The Brigade's major contribution to the operation was the use of long range reconnaissance patrols in this suspected enemy sanctuary. The patrols were made more difficult by the shortage of good water in the patrol area. In July, the lst Brigade moved to the Dak To area to find the 24th NVA Regiment. Extensive patrolling between Dak To and the Laotian border by LRRP teams produced only light enemy contact and only one air assault was made, when a long range reconnaissance patrol developed a possible contact north of Dak To. The 2\502 made a sweep but no enemy contact was developed.

One of the best stories of LRRP employment was told to the author by Major General Patrick during 1986. The general was commanding the 10!st Airborne Division in 1986 and was the guest speaker at the first LRRP reunion, which was held at Fort Campbell, Kentucky. On a tour of duty during the war in Vietnam, then Colonel Patrick, was the G-2 of the lst Air Cavalry Division. The division was heavily committed with all three of its combat brigades engaged in operations throughout its area of operations. There was some combat intelligence gathered that indicated there was an NVA Sapper Battalion of 900 men trying to slip into the division's area of operations. This sapper battalion was going to maneuver into position to attack the lightly defended division rear area headquarters. The only combat asset available to the G-2 section at that time was the Long Range Reconnaissance Patrol company. Colonel Patrick ordered the unit to deploy teams along the likely avenues of approach for the NVA

Colt 5.56MM CAR-15 Carbine

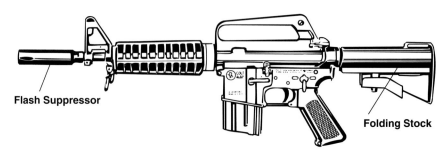

Flash Suppressor

Folding Stock

and find the enemy. On the third day of patrolling a team made contact with the NVA sapper unit as it worked its way toward their target. The team was instructed to shadow the sappers and report their progress. The team stayed with the NVA as they worked their way closer to the 1st Air Cavalry Division rear area. Two days after making contact with the enemy the team called to report that the sapper battalion had stopped and was making preparations to launch the attack. The team was instructed to stay in place and report when the enemy moved out to attack. After making that report the team was told they were to break contact and move out of the battle area to be picked up the next day. At 2300 hours the team called in on the radio of report the enemy was moving out for the attack, and the team was breaking contact. As the 900 enemy sappers moved quietly across the open area towards the 1st Cavalry Division's defense perimeter, all hell broke loose. The Klieg lights that had been set up on the defense line by the men of the division were turned on and truck mounted M16 quad .50 caliber machine guns opened fire. The fight was over quickly and a 900 man NVA sapper battalion was decimated, ending the threat to the base camp.

A team member makes a point during a premission briefing as the team prepares to go out on patrol. These men were assigned to the LRRP unit of the 1st Brigade, 101st Airborne during 1966. They are dressed in standard issue OD fatigues. (U.S. Army)

The Company F, 58th Infantry insignia sign was used to mark the company area. In early September the company moved to the west side of Camp Eagle to plug a weak spot in the division base camp's defense perimeter. The man along side the sign is SGT Brook, a member of the author's team. The mountains in the background led back to the Laos border area and our Area of Operations. (Author)

A team moves through a low area clearing, near the bottom of a valley, while on patrol. The blades of grass were as sharp as razor blades and would cut you twice as fast. The last man was the radio man, the short antenna for the backpack radio is visible over his right shoulder. The team is moving in a close file. (Author)

17

LRRPs in Vietnam - 1968

20 December 1967, saw the formal activation of the Long Range Reconnaissance Patrol companies for the U. S. Army in Vietnam. Each Army Division was assigned an Infantry Company with a headquarters section and two patrol platoons. The headquarters platoon had a supply section, radio section, operations section and a medic. The patrol platoons had a platoon leader, platoon sergeant, and eight six man patrols. The total authorized strength for a company was 118 men. The separate Army Infantry Brigades had a sixty-one man detachment that was broken down to a headquarters platoon and one patrol platoon. The two Field Forces, that were active in Vietnam, had a company in each Field Force that had 230 men with a headquarters section and four patrol platoons. During January of 1968 the last LRRP company, Company F, 58th Infantry (LRRP), was formed for the 101st Airborne Division which had just come into the country to link up with its lst Brigade, which had been in Vietnam since July of 1965.

When the numbers are all put together it's easy to see why the LRRPs were such an exclusive club. The total strength or head count for all of the LRRP companies in Vietnam was 1,530 men, of which there were 1,248 slots for the men who actual went out on patrol. Due to combat casualties and the Army's rotation policy there were never more that 900 men available in all of the LRRP companies in Vietnam to go out on missions on any given day. 1968 was the peak year for manpower in the Vietnam build-up with 586,000 men counted as being in the war zone.

The LRRP units in Vietnam were formed under the Table of Organization and Equipment number 7-157E dated 28 September 1964, with some modifications. The Transportation and Maintenance section and the Communications platoon were dropped because the teams would be using the division's assigned helicopters for all missions and they would only be using a short range voice radio, the AN PRC-25. The basic T 0 & E for a team on paper had a Staff Sergeant (E-6) as the team leader and a Sergeant (E-5) as the assistant team leader. There were two radio operators assigned to the team and both of them were supposed to be E-4s. The two Scouts in the team were also in the E-4 pay grade. The reality of war had most teams led by E-5s with E-4 as their assistants, with E-4s and E-3s filling the rest of the slots.

The primary mission for the team was reconnaissance behind the lines and since there weren't any lines in Vietnam the teams were put out in jungle areas where there weren't any friendly troops to find the enemy. The typical mission would last six days with the team working an A0 (Area of Operations) that was two kilometers wide and four kilometers long as the primary patrol area. There was a one kilometer band around the A0 that was a no fire zone for the artillery since we always operated in free fire zones. This type of set up was used so the artillery could keep firing their nightly H & I fire that had been pre-planned for the area weeks in advance. This use of artillery fire during the mission would help fool the enemy and make him think no one was in his back yard.

A mission would begin with a warning order given the day before the mission was to start. This warning order would tell the team leader where he was going, which map sheets would be used, and any intelligence on the enemy that was available for his area of operation. The team leader would alert the team and start his planning which included a map study to pick out the route to follow on the mission, an overlay of the route through the area for the operations section, pre-plotted artillery fire for emergency use, and an over flight to check the insertion landing zone. The assistant team leader would draw rations, special equipment, and

Team members board a UH-1 for an over flight to see if the Landing Zones (LZs) picked for the mission are actually useable. Many times the area looked good on the map, but when the over flight was made during the planning phase, the LZ was not open enough for the insertion. (John Looney)

The door gunner's view out of the insertion helicopter. The chopper is making its turn to line up with the one ship Landing Zone (LZ) in the jungle below. The LRRP team is ready to start their mission and will exit the Huey on the run. The door gun is a M-60 7.62MM machine gun. (Author)

(Above & Left) The author was bringing up the rear of the team line and was carrying the spare team PRC-25 radio. He was equipped with an M-16 rifle, which has a dust cover over the muzzle and a cleaning rod taped to the stock. The cleaning rod was used to clear jammed rounds. He carries a smoke grenade on the left harness strap and below it is a first aid pouch that contained a pen flare gun and extra flares. The heavy glove was used to clear vines and thorn branches from his path. During 1968 LRRPs cound not get the Black Army issue glove shell so they had to make do with heavy repelling gloves, it took a few trips into the field before the White glove was broke in enough to allow it to take the camouflage grease paint. (U.S. Army)

While moving up a rocky hillside, the team heard noise and stopped to listen. The Army photographer, who was along to record the mission, thought this would be a great time for a shot so he moved up quickly and snapped some pictures. SP/4 Taylor's expression reveals that he really did not feel that this was a good time for this. After the team cleared the area SGT Brooks had a long talk with the photographer about doing anything he wasn't told to do. (U.S. Army)

SP/4 Taylor was the team's point man for this patrol. Even while on break for the noon radio situation report (sitrep) he remains watchful. On the right side of his pistol belt is a white phosphorus (WP) grenade. Most team members carried at least one of these since they came in handy for breaking contact with an enemy force or for marking a target location. The large canaster on his web rear strap is an Albumin blood expander kit. (U. S. Army)

supervise the other team members equipment preparation. The R.T.0. (radio telephone operator) would draw the radios and the extra batteries needed for the mission and they would also get the secret radio codes (SOI) to be used on the mission. The whole team was a flurry of action cleaning and checking weapons, packing gear, reloading all of their M-16 magazines and getting ready for the mission briefing after the over flight.

Most missions started with a first light insertion in the mornings. This would give the team the best chance of getting put on the ground undetected and in case of an emergency the most daylight time to escape and evade the enemy. The insertion or extraction of a team required the use of five helicopters. There was one UH-1D Huey used as the command and control ship, another for the insertion ship, another as the chase ship, and two AH-1 Hueycobras for gun support just in case the team made contact during the insertion. The chase ship was used to help fool any ground observer who might see the insertion. The chase ship would fly low over the insertion ship, which was on the ground unloading, and pull up. The insertion ship would come up behind the chase ship and they would both fly away. To an enemy on the ground it would look like two helicopters had just swooped down to look and didn't land or unload. On an extraction, the chase ship was a spare in the case of a normal extraction or it

would carry the second set of ropes in case there was a need for a MacGuire extraction. The insertion and extraction were the two most dangerous times in a mission. Once on the ground the team would stay near the insertion Landing Zone (LZ) for thirty minutes to make sure the team had not been spotted. The helicopters would move off to another area and orbit until the patrol team leader called the C & C ship and released them. Once the team leader was ready to start the mission, the team would form a file and move out on the pre-planned heading.

An important part of every day on a mission was the radio report, made three times a day, to the tactical control center. This report was called a situation report (Sit Rep). Sit Reps were kept short and a typical report would go, " Normal Credit 5 Normal Credit 5 this is Normal Credit 21 Normal Credit 21, over." "Normal Credit 21 this is Normal Credit 5, over." Normal Credit 5 this is Normal Credit 21 Sit Rep Situation normal location Grape 8, moving Grape 4,

SGT Brooks assists SP/4 Harris up one of the steep hills the team encountered on their mission. On Harris' ruck sack are two smoke grenades and the radio antenna is visible running down the back of the ruck sack. He carries a two quart bladder type canteen on his pistol belt and has a knife strapped to his leg. (U. S. Army)

The third stream to cross in as many days. SP/4 Taylor crossed last on this one, since he was taking a break off point. On the forward hand guard of his M-16 was a strip of heavy Green tape used to break up the outline and serve as a kind of camouflage. He carries a standard issue Army survival knife taped to the harness of his web gear. (U. S. Army)

21

Another stream to cross. SP\4 Taylor starts out of the stream while the author is close behind to give him a push up the bank. On the authors ruck sack is a one quart canteen, a claymore mine and a two quart canteen on the far side. This ruck sack is attached to a cut down G. I. ruck sack frame. Whether or not to use a frame was up to the individual trooper. Over the author's right shoulder is the radio handset cord while the antenna is tied down on the far side of the pack. (U. S. Army)

out." When there was bad weather or there was a long distances between the radios, that could affect the radio reception or interrupt the radio transmission, the LRRP company would put a radio relay team out on a nearby firebase to make sure the patrol team had around the clock radio contact.

Claymore Anti-personnel Mine

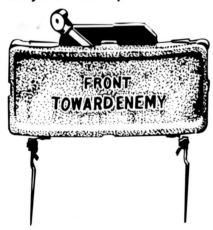

On some missions the hunting was good and plenty of signs of enemy activity were found. On rare instances the team would hold up and sent a smaller patrol out to check out good leads and collect information. During these side trips it helped to know that the rest of the team was guarding the trail in back of you so the enemy couldn't sneak behind you while you were trying to sneak up behind him.

A LRRP had to be able to read the signs and signals of the North Vietnamese Army (NVA) and Viet Cong (VC). The best weapons a LRRP had were a keen sense of observation and patience. If there were gun shots fired near a team no one would return the fire. It was a good

The author arrives back at base camp after a five day mission. On the right hand harness strap above the can is the strobe light that all team members carried. Tied on top of the ruck sack is the claymore mine carried by each team member on patrol, and a 57MM recoiless rifle round found on the mission. The plan was to drop the round from the extraction ship on the way back to Camp Eagle, but I forgot. (Author)

bet the enemy was reconning the area by fire and trying to get the team to expose its location by their return fire. A cigarette butt that hadn't turned brown by getting wet from the dew would help tell how long ago the enemy had been in the area. The NVA were good soldiers, but they could get careless and leave plenty of signs that told us they were around. The NVA and VC had a number of standard trail signs they would use when their soldiers thought they were in a safe area. All members of the team needed to understand these signs so we would know what the enemy was up to in that area. These signs would point out things like the placement of booby traps, directions to medical treatment areas, and the location of a water or a food cache.

LRRPs At Home

The LRRP Companies were stationed in the divisions main base camp and were assigned the secondary mission of being an on-call light infantry company for the base camp defense. They also had a section of the base camp defense perimeter which they were responsible for and, in many cases, helped build.

SSGT Phillip Byron, the author's old team leader, welcomed him back to base camp with a hot orange drink after a successful mission. Byron was rotating back to the states in a couple of days, and Team 9, call sign Normal Credit 21, had been turned over to the author. (Author)

Behind SSGT Byron on the left, is a good example of our sandbag work. Each Platoon tent was dug in by placing it in a hole that the engineers had carved in the hard earth with their bulldozers. The men then built up a three foot blast wall of sandbags all the way around the tent. (Author)

A lot of sandbags were used to protect the troop living area. The three small tents were for the officers and their rocket shelter can be seen behind the third tent. Camp Eagle was only a few months old at this time and the troops had not had the time to add the "comforts of home". (Author)

When the teams weren't out on missions there was a world of details to work on. We had to fill sandbags to put around the tents and bunkers, clean the latrines and build new defenses for the division base camp. The units were always training or testing new ideas when the time and equipment allowed. The more the men trained the better they could do their job. We also worked on training the helicopter pilots and crew men on the various extraction methods. When the time was available we would work with the different artillery units stationed near the base camp and practice adjusting artillery fire.

The men in the LRRP companies lived the best they could and took advantage of what creature comforts could be scraped up to make their rear area homes more comfortable. The

Our open air shower! This was not a true marvel of advanced engineering, but it got the job done. It was a good thing that there was no such thing as a modest LRRP. More than once a good shower was interrupted by incoming NVA 122MM rockets, and it was always good for a laugh to watch a man leave the shower on the run and dive into the rocket bunker. (Author)

A crashed Bell UH-1D Huey on the company helipad. This ship had less than 100 hours flight time and was brought down by a mechanical malfunction. All on board escaped with no injuries but the ship was totaled. The rotor blade and assorted parts tore down a few tents and there were a few near misses. (Author)

This was our supply tent in the new company area. On the horizon is Mount Nui Ke. The NVA and VC would set 122MM rackets on the slopes of the mountain and use our company area as their aiming point. The main helicopter refueling area was just over the hill from our area and the Army had put a large White panel in our company area to guide the choppers in to land. The company pulled a number of missions on Nui Ke and most of them were hot contact missions. (Author)

South Vietnamese would take used American artillery shell storage boxes and build foot lockers to sell to the Army P X located an the base. The men would buy the foot lockers for a few dollars and then they would have a place they could lock up their personal belongings when they were out on a mission. The men of the division and brigade LRRP unit were always a little jealous of the Field Force LRRP companies. The men of the 1st and 2nd Field Force lived like kings compared to our humble digs. The Field force men lived in buildings with concrete floors, wall lockers and bunks.

There were exciting days in the rear when a helicopter would crash near your tent or a big enemy sapper attack was headed your way, and there were a few quiet and boring days when the best you could do was take a few pictures to send home and read a book. Once in a while there was a trip to the beach with a beer bust and cookout to help us relax. One of the highlights of the year in the base camp of the 101st Airborne Division was the completion of the ice plant built by the Seebees. In mid-September we got the first block of ice into the compa-

The author was a LRRP team leader in Vietnam. He carries a bandoleer across his chest with seven loaded twenty-round M16 magazines, a strobe light taped to the web gear on his left shoulder, a smoke grenade on his right shoulder, and the team's PRC-25 radio. The M16 has a cleaning rod taped to it for use in quickly clearing jams.

A Long Range Recon Patrol (LRRP) team leader from the 1st Infantry Division, calls a halt while crossing a dike in a rice paddy during May of 1967. He is carrying a CAR-15, the folding stock carbine variant of the M16 rifle.

This LRRP team member is armed with a Swedish K, 9mm submachine gun that is equipped with a sound suppressor. The weapon is non-standard and was supplied to the LRRPs by the Army Special Forces.

SP-4 Harris covers a suspected Viet Cong 122mm rocket launching site while the author watches the site for VC activity. The previous day, the VC had fired a number of rockets from this area and the LRRP team was called in to investigate the launch site.

BGEN Willard Pearson briefs members of the 1st Brigade, 101st Airborne Division, Provisional LRRP unit prior to a mission during June of 1966. The men are armed with early M16 rifles with three prong flash suppressors and are carrying Second World War vintage grenades. All have new issue "Tiger" stripe camouflage uniforms drawn from the Special Forces.

One of the machine gun bunkers we built in our sector of the base camp defensive perimeter. The opening in the center is the firing port for an 7.62ᴍᴍ M-60 machinegun. (Author)

7.62ᴍᴍ M-60 Machinegun

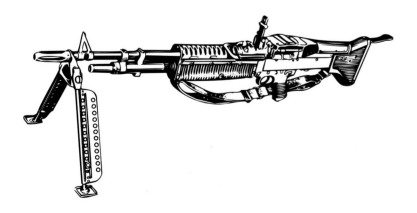

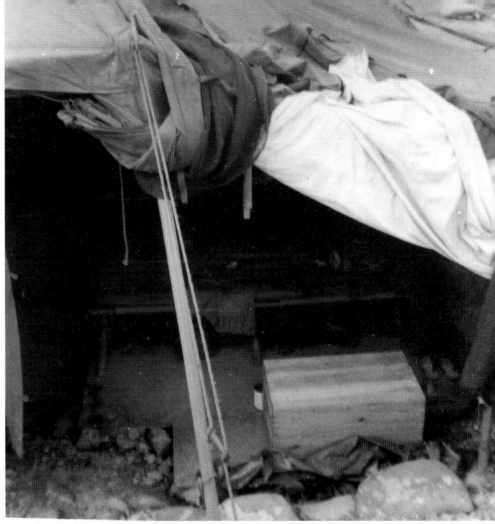

There's no place like home, the wooden box was a footlocker made by the local Vietnamese from our artillery ammunition boxes. We could buy them in the camp PX. As long as it didn't rain we were just fine, but when it rained everything flooded if the drain hole got plugged. The last thing we did before going out on a mission was put all of our belongings up on the cot. Many times we came home to wet gear when both teams would be out on missions and no one in operations remembered to come to our tent and check the drain hole. (Author)

ny. Each unit was allocated one block a day. The LRRP Company didn't have a mess hall and we ate with the 17th Cav, so we took our ice to the small clubhouse we built, scrounged up a cooler and set up shop. The men pooled their resources, bought beer and pop to stock the cooler and, from that day forward, you could go to the club and get a cold beer or pop for a dime. When a team came back from a mission they were allowed one free cold drink on the house. There weren't any rank barriers at the LRRP club.

There was an ever-present danger in all of the base camps throughout Vietnam from the enemy forces that roamed the various divisions rear areas almost at will. Some days we would

The author and SSGT Byron sitting on the rocket shelter at the base camp of the 101st Airborne Division, Camp Eagle, during July of 1968. The base was located near Phu Bia in I Corp, South Vietnam. This was the cemetery for the city of Hue and was near the old Imperial tombs. Many of the tents were next to huge family graves and we used them for cover during rocket attacks. (Author)

be hit with sniper fire or a ground attack that would probe the outpost line. On other days we would receive a rocket or mortar attack. These attacks could last a few minutes or an hour, it just depended on how the enemy's ammo was holding out that day.

After the 1968 bombing halt, called by President Johnson to promote the peace talks, the number of rocket attacks in the I Corp tactical zone showed a dramatic increase in number, as the NVA took advantage of the lull in the air war to ship more ammunition south. The I Corp tactical zone was at the head of the Ho Chi Minh trail and we always got the fresh NVA troops and new supplies first.

While out on patrol a LRRP team had more to worry about than just the enemy. There were times when American forces poised a greater threat. Most U. S. Army aviation units would fly a reconnaissance team out in the free fire zones to look for enemy activity. These teams were called "Hunter-Killer Teams." In the 101st they were called Pink Teams. The idea was

SSG Philip Byron , SP\4 Evans, PFC Munoz building sand bag and sheet metal bunkers. The Army can always find constructive work for LRRPs between missions. Building bunkers and filling sandbags were the two most boring details we had; but when the B-40 rockets rained in we were very happy to have spent the time. Steel runway planking and sand bags were the building material of choice. (Author)

the OH-6A light observation helicopter (LOH) would fly low to look for enemy troops or draw enemy ground fire. If the LOH spotted something the two AH-1G Cobra gunships would come down to destroy the target. The lack of coordination between the aviation units and the LRRP companies was a real sore point with many LRRPS.

The men of the LRRP companies never wore regular uniforms on missions. The author used to wear an NVA shirt and Ho Chi Minh sandals on missions. Tiger stripes were a favorite uniform for patrols. We didn't carry regular American rucksacks and many times we had unusual weapons and web gear. There were a few times when a Pink Team would spot a LRRP team moving and mistake them for NVA troops. The helicopter team was on a different radio frequency than the LRRP team so no radio contact could be made. To fire a pen gun flare as a signal was a sure ticket to getting fired up by the Cobras. The only way a team could hope to save itself was to hear the ships coming in and take off their hats and look up. We had to hope the pilots would take the time to look and see we weren't NVA. All team members had an orange flash panel sewn into the inside of their hat and would hold the hat up and push the panel out to be seen. The worst move a team could make was to run for cover.

The Army introduced a new camouflage uniform for LRRP units during 1968. This uniform was called the random leaf pattern uniform. The men of the LRRP companies called this uniform the "Flower Power." The use of the new uniform helped with the pilot identification problem but old habits die hard and many men clung to the tiger stripes. The author does not doubt that many helicopter pilots had second thoughts about picking up the five or six LRRPs who would run out onto the extraction LZ and jump on board their ships. If the extraction was on a hot LZ the pilots never knew for sure whether they were picking up a LRRP team or being charged by a force of enemy troops. To add to the problem the NVA did try to lure helicopters into the wrong LZ using captured U. S. radios and captured smoke grenades to match the identification smoke thrown by a team. The problem got so bad that the pilots would tell us to pop a smoke but not say which color. We would pick the color of the smoke grenade to throw and the pilot would identify the color and wait for us to "roger" his ID.

The primary mission of the Long Range Reconnaissance Patrol Company was to field a six

This is a hunter killer helicopter team which consisted of an OH-6A observation ship and two AH-1G Hueycobra gunships. We called them Pink Teams and while they were good at their job of visual reconnaissance they did cause problems for the LRRP teams on missions when they mistook LRRPs for the enemy. (U.S. Army)

The primary insurtion/extraction vehicle used in Vietnam consisted of various models of the Bell UH-1 Huey turbine helicopter. The UH-1 could carry the six man team and their equipment into a patrol area and could, if need be, extract a team under fire. (Tim Kerr)

man reconnaissance team into enemy territory. This team would stay in the area of operations for six days and follow a pre-planned route through the A 0. This route was laid out to allow the team to investigate all of the likely areas that would be of interest to the Army intelligence units. The team was to check map accuracy, look for trails, check possible base camp locations, record enemy movement in the A 0 and note the thickness of the jungle canopy as they moved. The mission was considered a success if the team could avoid enemy contact for the six days of the mission and get out quietly without tipping the enemy off to the fact he had been checked out.

The missions weren't as easy as they sound and there were a number of factors that came into play on every mission. There was a constant shortage of men in the units and most LRRP companies never were close to full strength. It became the norm to use a five man team and a few missions were pulled with a four man team. There were never any real long range reconnaissance patrols pulled with less than four men. The Army didn't send lone soldiers out on missions although it does make for some great bar-room story telling. On one of the missions that the author was on, the Army sent a combat photographer to take a few pictures. Our team was scheduled out for a six day mission west of fire base Birmingham in the 101st Airborne's A 0. We only had four men for this mission so we told the photographer he could go along but he had to carry a weapon and he would have to stay out for the full mission. He said that was

A LRRPs best friend isn't a dog; its a snake. This Bell AH-1G Hueycobra is lifting off after refueling and rearming before escorting an insertion ship out on a mission. The gunships always tried to have as much fuel on board as possible for an insertion in case they had to make gun runs to support a hot extraction if the enemy was waiting when the team set down.

OK with him so we showed him how to pack a rucksack and loaned him some web gear and a uniform. After the first day I know he wished he had said no, but he hung in there and completed the mission. We were lucky that we didn't make contact on the mission but there were a few close brushes. Much to his credit the combat photographer did a good job in the field and we offered him a permanent slot with us after the mission.

There were times when the LRRP teams were used as force expanders. The long range reconnaissance patrol teams could cover a large area by being sent out in adjoining A 0s. Six teams working together could cover more area in six days than a regular Army battalion could, and we required the use of less assets and support. It made good sense to put a six man LRRP team into a suspected enemy base camp area without an artillery prep and only use a few helicopters. If the area was occupied by the enemy, a team could check the area out and the Division Commander could plan an operation that would allow the U. S. forces to have the upper hand. If the area was empty the Army would have saved a lot of time and effort and the

Before going out on his next patrol, the author posed for a photo to send home. He is carrying full field gear consisting of a standard ammo pouch full of M-16 magazines on the right side of his pistol belt, a one quart canteen, a canteen cover full of M-16 magazines and another canteen cover containing five fragmentation grenades. On the right side of his web gear is taped a can of Albumin blood expander and on the left harness is taped a smoke grenade. He also carried a Bowie knife with the scabbard taped to his web gear harness. He preferred this knife to the standard Army survival knife. When actually going on patrol, his sleeves would be rolled down and the civilian watch would be left behind in his footlocker. (Author)

troops could be better used elsewhere.

In October of 1968 the 1st Cavalry Division (Air Mobile) was moved from I Corp south to the III Corp area. The 101st Airborne had to cover two full A Os until another unit was deployed to that region. The division commander made full use of his LRRP company during that period and maintained heavy patrol activity in the extra A 0. On one of those missions the author was leading a team on the Laotian border and found a major base camp. The NVA unit that built the camp was out of the area and the team was able to check out one third of the area covered by the bunker and living quarters. We found radios, weapons, and the rucksack of the Mien 6B Battalion Commander. In the rucksack was a picture of the battalion commander in dress whites standing beside his wife and child, a package of letters from some eastern block countries, a shirt, and an NVA battle flag. The team also got to study the construction of the living areas and a cooking area with a stove made of baked clay. The stove had a smoke dispersal tunnel that was dug up the side of the ridge line and emptied into a large pit with interwoven branches over it to hide the smoke. The team was pulled out on the second day and an infantry company with an attached engineer platoon came in to relieve us and to blow up the base camp. On the second day that the infantry company was in the area the NVA unit came back and a major battle was fought over the next two days. There weren't many missions when a team didn't find some signs of the enemy.

There were times when the weather could be our worst enemy. When most people think of Vietnam it is from the reference point of tropical jungle and heat, but in I Corp in the winter months, it got cold at night. We all carried a poncho that the 5th SF group bought for their native troops to use and it was issued to the LRRP Companies too. We would sew half of an American poncho liner inside our poncho and that was our sleeping cover. When a team stopped for the night each man got down in place and then moved any sticks and twigs that would make noise if we rolled over on them in our sleep. That was our home. We would place our rucksack by our head, crawl out fifteen feet and place our claymore mines, keep our web gear on, lay down, cover ourselves with the poncho, pull our rifle in close and go to sleep until our guard shift came around. We always slept within easy reach of each other and no one got up during the night to answer the call of nature. We were issued an Army jungle sweater for use when we slept, and we carried that in the winter months. We would take off the web gear, put on the sweater, then put the web gear back on for the night. If it was raining, then we got wet and cold, if it wasn't raining then we just got cold.

Rain, fog, and low ceilings took there toll on the nerves of the men on missions. During rainstorms the radio reception was cut down and many times the moisture would affect the radios and they would quit working. The fog could delay an insertion and the longer a chopper spent in the area the more likely the enemy was to figure out something was up. If the insertion ship could get the team in and trouble broke out the gunships would have a hard time giving fire support. The extra time in the air going out to the A 0 would mean less fuel for both the insertion ship and the gunships so they couldn't stick around and get us out in an emergency. There were times when the mountains of I Corp would be socked in for days, and we couldn't expect our pilots to fly out in a cloud through the mountains to come help us.

Bowie Knife and Scabbard

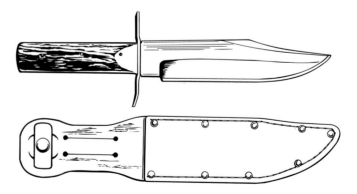

A LRRP with the PRC-25 Field Radio. This man has a short antenna on the radio and has not pulled the antenna down to help hide the fact that he is a radioman. An antenna stuck up in the air like that makes this man a good target for enemy troops. It was impossible to move through thick jungle quietly with an antenna deployed and knocking around. (U.S. Army)

When the weather went bad we knew we were on our own.

It is hard to imagine what it feels like to be soaking wet for six days with no way to get dry for even a few minutes. The cold and wet go all the way to the bone, and your hands and feet look like prunes. We tried to carry a couple of extra pair of socks, but they were wet in seconds after you changed them and put your wet boots back on. Our hands would get so stiff that it was hard to do a simple act like un-button the fly on our pants.

During the summer months we still had the rain and fog but then the heat was the problem. Each member of the team carried salt tablets to help prevent heat stroke, and we took up to ten tablets a day. The sweat would wash the camouflage paint off our faces in a few minutes and we were forced to put our face back on again at every break. By the second day our uniforms would be white on the back and under the arms with crusted salt. In the jungle the high humidity and crushing heat sapped the body of any energy. Each man carried an equipment load that weighed close to eighty pounds, and to get up off the ground after a break one man would have to help the other men up and then get his gear put on and be helped up. At the end of a day's march there wasn't a man who had any trouble going to sleep.

A radioman makes contact with base for the team's required Situation Report (SITREP) if a team was out of contact for three SITREPs, it was declared Missing In Action. The normal requirement was for three reports per day while in the field. (U.S Army via Jim Mesko)

SP\4 Harris working on a meal. The canteen cup is held over a ball of burning C-4 plastic explosive. The C-4 burned with a pale blue flame and gave off no smoke or strong smell to give the patrol's position away. A ball of C-4 the size on a large marble would boil a cup of water in a minute. (Author)

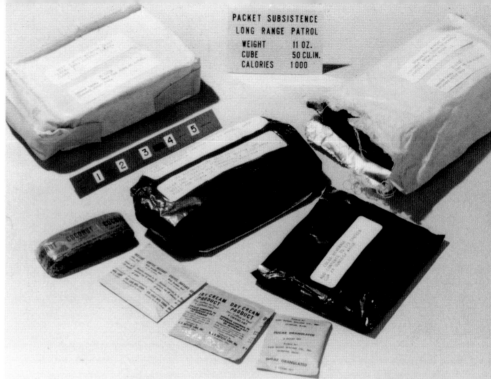

The new " Packet Subsistence, Long Range Patrol" ration that was under development by the food division of the U. S. Army Natick Laboratories of the Materiel Command. This division conducts food research, packing, packaging, and related programs for the armed forces. The two rations shown here are the main courses, beef with rice and spaghetti with meat sauce. The other items are cereal bars, coffee, cocoa, sugar and cream. The precooked, dehydrated items are reconstituted by adding hot water. (U.S. Army)

Insects were always a problem, rain or shine, and the one thing we hated the worst were the ground leeches. When we took a break we could sit and watch the leeches race towards us. A leech could get on a person and crawl all over their body without the person knowing they were there. When a leech bit you couldn't feel it, and the only way you knew a leech was on you was when a fellow team member would spot a large bulge under your uniform. The leech would drink his fill of blood and drop off the man as he walked. Every night when we would powder our feet the tops of our socks would be stiff with our dried blood. One time I counted seventeen leeches on my legs at the top of my boots. We would soak our boots and pants legs with insect repellent to stop the leeches but it wore off in two days and the smell would carry through the jungle and be a dead give-a-way of our presence.

The Long Range Reconnaissance Patrol companies weren't issued a lot of special equipment. We got our poncho, rucksack, and tiger stripe uniforms from the 5th Special Forces. The companies were allocated a larger share of the short barreled collapsible stock M-16 rifle that we called the CAR-15 or XM-177 rifle, but the officers always got first choice even though they didn't go on patrol. There were some items that were standard issue for our men that weren't issued to regular line company infantrymen. Each team member got a U.S. Army survival knife, a strobe light, serum albumin (a blood expander), a special survival kit, and a

AK-47 Assault Rifle

signal mirror. Of course we had access to the full range of weapons that were available in Vietnam, such as LAW rockets, M-79 40MM grenade launchers, M-60 machine guns and anything else we might have needed. Most of the time we just carried M-16s, CAR-15s, pistols, claymore mines, and grenades.

The use of captured enemy equipment was limited in 1968. The AK-47 was still in short supply and wasn't carried on missions. The use of HO CHI MINH sandals in the field wasn't widely accepted but they were used. The sandal wasn't good to walk in but if a man had to

VC Spike Booby Trap

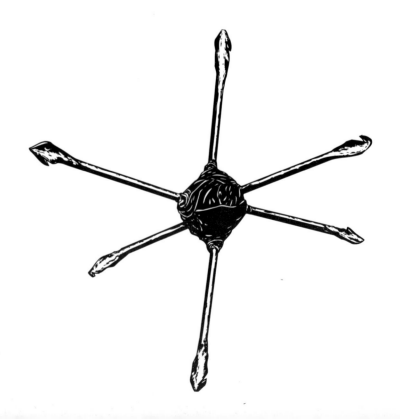

A collection of enemy weapons captured in a major field operation by the 173rd Airborne Brigade. The round device in the foreground is the Chinese version of the claymore mine. It weighs about forty pounds and was a deadly weapon to face. Also in the collection are SKS rifles, AK-47 assault rifles, mortar, and RPGs (Rocket Propelled Grenades). (U.S. Army)

Checking out a high speed trail. After a complete recon of the area a LRRP takes a look at a well used VC/NVA trail while taking advantage of a nearby small stream to resupply his water. While checking out enemy trails, LRRPs had to be always on the lookout for booby traps. (Author)

34

A M-16AI and a CAR 15, the short carbine variant of the M-16. Many of the men in the company carried the CAR 15 because it was easy to handle in the jungle and less likely to get caught on vines and undergrowth. The author always carried the old reliable long rifle on patrol. Both weapons used the same ammunition and magazines. (Author)

Two LRRPs wait for the order to move out to an ambush site. SP/4 Sanez checks his CAR-15 rifle while SP/4 Meszaros fights off boredom. This period was the beginning of the mis-use of the LRRP assets. The teams were pulled off reconnaissance missions and were being used more often for ambush missions. (Author)

A LRRP stands guard while other members of the team rest along a jungle trail. Even while resting, they had to remain always alert to prevent being spotted by the enemy. The heat and high humidity of the jungle made frequent rest stops a necessity. (U.S. Army via Jim Mesko)

35

Members of a LRRP unit prepare to go out on patrol. The man in the center is the team radio man. There is an AK-47 assault rifle leaning against the wall at the right. It was unusual for LRRPs to carry enemy weapons in the field. (U.S. Army via Jim Mesko)

LRRP Pistols

Colt M1911 .45 Caliber Semi-Automatic

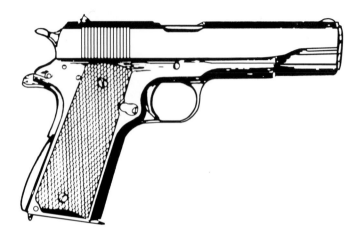

Browning 9MM Semi-Automatic

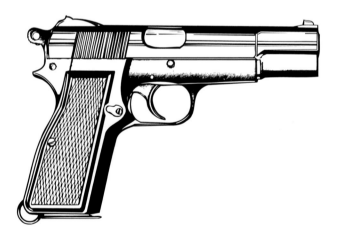

cross a trail or use a trail, the sandal would allow the foot print to blend in rather than leave the distinct G.I. boot print. The author used sandals on a number of missions with good results. Some times we would use captured enemy clothing to help disguise the fact that we were U. S. troops. There were many times when an enemy soldier or group of soldiers would walk right up to a team and shout a greeting. We almost always got off the first shot in any encounter with enemy forces.

The second most favorite weapon of LRRPs was the claymore mine. We all carried one of them on every mission and set them out when we stopped for the night. The claymore gave us a light area weapon that could be employed in a number of different ways. We would use them to set an ambush, lay a booby trap, and with a hand grenade we could set it to help a team break contact with the enemy. The author liked to hook claymore mines together with detonating cord to make a daisy chain ambush. When the main cap was fired all of the mines that were hooked together would explode simultaneously. This set up would allow a team to expand its kill zone to fool the enemy about the size of the force that ambushed them. A daisy chain was easy to make using non electric blasting caps and det cord. The construction of a daisy chain ambush in the field did require a steady hand, and some tender loving care.

The teams used the standard PRC-25 FM field radio on all missions. Since we kept both radios on 24 hours a day during the mission we had to change the batteries every other day. Each radioman had his full load of equipment, the radio and a spare battery. All the other

A Bell UH-1D Dustoff Medevac helicopter of the 15th Medical Battalion, 1st Cavalry Division (Airmobile) hovers over the jungle canopy while the crewman lowers a jungle penetrator down for pickup of a wounded man. The prongs of the penetrator folded down to act as a seat for the individual being picked up. During these medevac pickups both the helicopter and team were wide open for enemy attack. (U.S. Army)

A wounded man is hoisted on board the UH-1D Dustoff Medevac helicopter via the jungle penetrator. Quick medical evacuation of a wounded man could make the difference in life or death. The jungle penetrator was the best way to pluck a wounded man from the thick jungle terrain. (U. S. Army)

The United States Navy hospital ship USS SANCTUARY (AH-17) at anchor in the harbor at Da Nang, South Vietnam, on 2 July 1970. Many critically wounded men were evacuated straight to the hospital ship from the battle field, saving their lives. The SANCTUARY was a fully equipped floating hospital with seventy-four beds (expandable to 300 in an emergency). She was fully staffed with fifty-five medical officers, six dental corps officers, twenty-one medical service officers, 177 nurse corps officers, 583 enlisted medical personnel and the ships crew of eleven officers and 235 enlisted men. The ship had facilities including twelve operating rooms, four X-ray rooms, intensive care unit and burn unit. She had a helicopter platform capable of handling up to and including CH-47 Chinook medium lift helicopters. After a long career, SANCTUARY was decommissioned on 28 March 1974 and she joined the National Defense Reserve Fleet (mothball fleet) in the James River, Virginia.

team members got stuck carrying extra radio batteries too, but there never was a lot an complaining about the extra weight.

The real highlight of being in a LRRP company was the freeze dried food. These meals were recognized as the best in the Army, and had a trade ratio of three to one with C-rations. The meals were developed for the Army by the Oregon Freeze Dry food company and were tested by the U. S. Army in 1964. There were eight different meals. We had Chicken Stew, Chicken Rice, Beef Stew, Beef Rice, Beef Hash, Pork and Scalloped potatoes, Chile con carne, and Spaghetti.

Oregon Freeze Dry got it's first order for rations in 1966 and produced 1.8 million meals under that contract. There was a follow up contract for 6.5 million meals in 1987 and the company produced 9.6 million meals in 1967. At peak production they made 65,000 meals a day. The cost of a meal started at $1.70 each in 1966 and was down to $.87.8 each by 1970. The fright cost for a single meal to Vietnam was $.04.5. The last contract for this popular meal was awarded in 1983.

The bombing halt was in full swing by October of 1968 and the North Vietnamese Army had started to recover from the beating it took during the TET offensive. The base camp of the 101st was receiving rocket attacks on a regular basis. In the other parts of the country the same pattern of stepped up attacks was being followed. The election was near and all of the American commanders knew the shape of the war was going to change. To counter the increase in enemy activity and relieve the chronic shortage of fighting manpower, the LRRP companies were pushed into the gap. The basic reconnaissance mission was put aside for a more active role by the teams. There was a growing frustration among the team members at not being able to strike back at the enemy. There were many times when a team had to sit quietly and let fat targets pass by. The "Body Count Syndrome" was taking hold, and the natural aggressiveness of the young and well trained LRRPs was starting to chew at their good judgment. There were increasing cases of contact with the enemy and it wasn't all caused by the increasing numbers of enemy troops in the field. Slowly the officers in the companies started to increase missions into hotter areas and encourage the team leaders to be more aggressive, pull prisoner snatch missions, and set up ambushes.

In the regular infantry most ambushes were pulled in close proximity to the main body of the infantry company, and help was never far away if the ambush went sour. The LRRP companies would field a six or twelve man team to go out on patrol and set up an ambush during the third and fourth day of the mission. We were always miles from the nearest friendly infantry units and didn't have good support. The teams did have the element of surprise on

SGT John Looney and one of his team members putting up the AN-986A/6 antenna mast at a fire base before the patrols are inserted into the area of operations (AO). The radio relay would go out one day before a mission was started, to get set up and be ready to receive messages at the time of insertion. (John Looney)

An unknown LRRP radio relay team member has climbed up the antenna mast to make last minute adjustments to Sgt Looney's equipment. The mast was held steady by two lines. The heavy line coming down was the transmission cable. (John Looney)

The radio relay team of Company L, 75th Rangers. All radio relay men had field experience as LRRPs. Since the radio relay was often the only link between the LRRP team on patrol and help in the event of hot contact. SGT Looney's (center) team consisted of Rufus, Walker, Van Lueven and Wilkes. (John Looney)

A fighting position used by the radio relay team during their stay on Firebase Eagle's Nest. The radio team was supporting two LRRP teams who were running sperate missions at the upper end of the valley. In the event of an enemy attack the team would use this position to fight from. (John Looney)

Firebase Eagle's Nest was located in the upper end of the A Shau valley. The area around the firebase was kept stripped of cover to prevent a surprise NVA sapper assault. Anyone attempting to reach the base had to cover the open areas around it. Across the valley from the base was the Laotian border. Visible in the upper right corner is the barrel of one of the base 155mm guns. (John Looney)

The author wearing a South Vietnamese poncho in a vain attempt to stay dry. On the sixth day of this particular mission the ceiling was up to fifty feet and the company commander sent out one last helicopter search mission. The team moved to the river and was able to signal the chopper and was sucessfully extracted. (Author)

Two LRRP team members take a break and check their equipment. One man is checking his snap ring on the web gear harness. The vines and brush in the jungle could strip equipment off a man faster that a big city pick pocket. (Author)

Four menbers of a five man patrol working the Roa La river on the north edge of the A Shau valley. Two LRRP teams had been inserted in adjoining Area of Operations (AOs) five days earlier, and the second team made contact with an enemy force and was shot out within the first hour. This team had to jump from the chopper on insertion because the ship couldn't land due to blown down trees. One radio was broken on insertion, and the other quit working on the second day. At the time this picture was taken the team had been out of contact for three days and was considered MIA. SP\4 Harris is holding his hat to catch the rain as a joke. It started to rain within hours of the insertion and didn't stop for all six days of the mission. (Author)

LRRP Support Weapons

M-72 Light Anti-Tank Weapon (LAW)

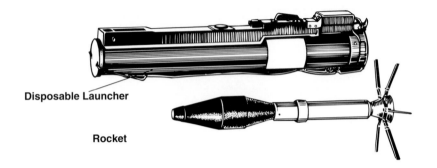

Disposable Launcher

Rocket

M-79 40mm Grenade Launcher

40mm Grenade

M67 90MM Shoulder Fired 90mm Recoiless Rifle

On ambushes, teams were often joined by other members of the division, who would provide heavy weapons support. This soldier is carrying an M-60 7.62mm machine gun and at least five belts of 7.62mm ammunition. (U.S. Army via Jim Mesko)

count due to the laxness of the enemy in his own stomping grounds. There were few times when the teams climbed on the back of the Tiger and got a surprise of their own.

The medical support for a LRRP team in contact was extremely limited. There wasn't a position for a medic to be assigned to a team and the one medic assigned to the company stayed at the base camp most of the time. The LRRPs were trained on basic medical procedure in RECONDO school and by the medic assigned to the company. The average LRRP team member was better trained in field medical work than the infantrymen assigned to the line companies of the various combat divisions in Vietnam. During the medical training phase of RECONDO school each man was trained to set and splint broken bones, treat and bandage a sucking chest wound, treat head wounds, and stop arterial bleeding. Each man had to learn how to draw blood from a fellow student so that in the field he could hit the vein in a man's arm or leg and start giving a wounded team member the serum albumin blood expanders intravenously. Quick action by fellow team members was the only medical help a wounded LRRP could expect on the ground.

There were times when a team was in contact with an enemy force and couldn't break contact because they had a critically wounded teammate that couldn't be moved. When that case arose, with the team being located in thick jungle, they would call for a UH-ID medevac helicopter with a jungle penetrator to come out and pick up the wounded man. The team would load the wounded team member on to the jungle penetrator, give as much cover fire as possi-

Larry Chambers fires his CAR-15 at North Vietnamese Army (NVA) troops that were hiding in a tree line. The enemy force tried to cut off the team, but quick action and air support allowed them to break contact. (Author)

The four NVA troops that came out the woodline after the team were quickly killed. The smoke is from a Yellow smoke grenade popped to mark our position for the helicopter gunships so they would not hits us during their gunruns. (Author)

"Contact, Contact I say again Contact," SP\4 Looney scrambles for new cover as he calls the TOC (Tactical Operations Center) after the team ran into an NVA line company in the woods. He is using a PRC-25 radio with a short antenna to report the problem and get gunship support. Tied to the radio is a claymore mine. The two men on the left flank check out the woodline where the enemy tried to out flank the team. (Author)

43

Now that the firefight is over and the extraction helicopter is on the way in, Larry Chambers is obviously releaved and happy to survive the fight. He has the carrying strap of his CAR-15 attached to the front sight post and uses the strap to help steady the weapon when firing. He also has colored tape applied around the foregrip to act as a camouflage and break up the solid Black color of the foregrip. (Author)

SP\4 Looney is talking on the PRC-25 to the extraction helicopter. He is carrying his CAR-15 and has a smile on his face as the UH-1 starts to make its approch to extract the team. (Author)

ble while the men was winched up to the helicopter. When the man was safe on the ship, and the chopper out of the area the team would then move to a safer location for extraction.

In the I and II Corp area a seriously wounded man with a life threatening wound could be flown out to the U. S. Navy hospital ship USS SANCTUARY for treatment. These ships were complete floating hospitals that cruised up and down the coastline of the two northern tactical control zones. The hulls of the hospital ships were painted white with large red crosses on the

side and they normally cruised twelve miles off the coast line to be out of the range of any enemy activity that could prove to be dangerous to the ship. The ship had a helipad on the rear deck that could accommodate the CH-47 Chinook helicopter.

Those men with non-life threatening wounds would go to the closet field medical center or MASH unit for classification for further evacuation or treatment. There were a number of large held hospitals located in Vietnam, and there were rehabilitation centers with each of them. Sometimes wounded men were evacuated out of the country to other U.S. hospitals located an the Pacific rim. During TET 1968 some casualties were evacuated all the way back to stateside hospitals due to the sudden overloading of the U.S. Army medical system during

This is a reflection of our feelings about both the area we we in and the mission we were assigned. This was an area of low scrub that was worked by wood cutters. The NVA would mix in with the wood cutters in the afternoon and infiltrate back towards Hue to pull a raid on an outpost. The LRRP team would watch the NVA come out and count them, if the odds were good we would ambush them the next morning when they came back. John Meszaros has a claymore bag hung over his sholder. SP\4 Sanez has a camo brert and Larry Chambers has one of the new baseball type hand grenade hung on his webb gear. (Author)

Captured equipmet was always welcomed by the intelligence groups. This is a Chinese made 12.7MM machine gun used as an anti-aircraft weapon. It was captured at an enemy base camp. This type of machine gun was particularly effective against low flying helicopters. (Joe Troxell)

With the extraction ship on the way in a LRRP fires his M-16 weapon after another team member had test fired an experimental weapon equipped with a sound supressor so we could compare the sound. The suppressor turned out to be not very quite and its shots sounded like a .22 caliber long rifle hunting weapon was being fired. There is a shell casing visible in the air just above the troopers hand. (Author)

When not out on missions, LRRP teams trained in patrol movements in areas near their base camps. This team was from the 25th Infantry Division based at Cu Chi. (U.S. Army)

the heavy fighting.

One of the most important sections of the Long Range Reconnaissance Patrol company was the radio relay group. This section was broken down into two support teams who's mission was to provide the team out on patrol a 24 hour radio link to the T 0 C (Tactical Operations Center). The PRC-25 radio that was standard team issue had an operational distance range of five miles (8 km) which varied with the weather and terrain conditions. For the teams that operated in the mountains and jungle of the I, II, and III TCZs maintaining radio contact could be a hit or miss proposition. During one situation report a team would be talking directly to the TOG; the next report would find the team out of contact or only able to receive and not transmit. There were times when a team would have to stop and wait while the radioman set up the long antenna to make contact. Many missions were so far out from the base camp TOC that the radio didn't have the range under ideal conditions to transmit back to the base.

The author checking out another high speed enemy trail, in his right hand is a candy bag dropped by a passing North Vietnamese Army trooper. The sugar inside the bag was dry and there were no ants, indicating that the the enemy had been in the area early that morning. These were some of the signs that LRRPs had to learn to read both to get an accurate picture of enemy movements and to stay alive. (Author)

The team waiting for the extraction ships. The author is talking to his radio man SP\4 Looney. On his hip is his non-issue knife, and the canteen cover is full of hand grenades. Behind Looney sits SP\4 Miller with a M-79 grenade launcher. The trooper with the helmet is from the air rifle platoon of 2\17th Cav. When we discovered that the food gathering group we had ambushed out numbered us three to one and had a NVA escort waiting we had to call for help from the air rifle platoon to bail us out. (Author)

A team on the move had to use the short three foot steel tape antenna on the radio. This antenna was for general short range work only, but it was the only antenna we could use that didn't catch every branch and vine as the radio operator tried to move quietly through the jungle. It was impossible for a team to move with the ten foot long sectional antenna attached to the radio and a team didn't have the time to change antennas in case of enemy contact. The radio relay teams were used to close the radio transmission gap and insure constant radio contact.

A relay team would move out to a fire base that was close to the operational area for the teams and set up an AT-984 A\G long wire multiple wavelength antenna to extend the range of their radios. The relay team had one of the most difficult jobs in the company. The relay teams were required to pull radio watch 24 hours a day for as long as the teams were out in the field. They suffered under some of the worst conditions and almost always ended up borrowing a fighting bunker from the unit attached to the fire base. The radio relay men were shelled more often on the fire bases and had to help fight off more enemy attacks than any team out on a mission.

Transition

Early in 1968, the Chairman of the Joint Chiefs of Staff recommended to Lyndon B. Johnson, then President of the United States, that 240,000 men of the National Guard and Reserve forces be called to active duty and deployed to Vietnam. Only 24,000 of the suggested 240,000 men were actually called to active duty. The only infantry unit included in the call up was Company D, 151st LRRP, 38th Infantry Division of the Indiana National Guard.

Company D, 151st LRRP was mobilized 13 May 1968, and sent to Fort Benning ,Georgia for six months of additional training before the unit was deployed to the war zone. The unit went to the Jungle Operations Center at Fort Gulick in the Panama Canal Zone for a three week jungle orientation course, during their Fort Benning training phase. In October of 1968, the unit was ordered to cut back to 214 men and prepare for overseas movement.

The advance party arrived in Vietnam in November of 1968 and was assigned to the Second Field Force stationed at Bien Hoa. The men of the advance party from D Company were merged with Company F, 51st LRRP and started to pull missions right away and the company took its first man killed in action (KIA) on 11 November 1968. The balance of D Company, 151st LRRP arrived in-country on 30 December 1968. The company received its Combat Infantry Badge streamer 8 March 1969, and was released from active duty during November of 1969. Company D, 151st LRRP was credited with four campaign streamers and the men were awarded over 500 individual awards and decorations.

January of 1969, saw the LRRP companies preparing for the change over to the Ranger company designation and the picking up of a new and more combat active mission profile. All Long Range Reconnaissance Patrol Companies would come under the 75th Infantry (Ranger) starting in February of 1969 except the 151st Infantry which would change from Company D, 151st Infantry, LRRP to Company D, 151st Infantry, Ranger. In November of 1969 when Company D, 151st was released from active duty, the Army activated Company D, 75th Infantry, Ranger to complete the LRRP reorganization.

A LRRP team from Company L, 75th Rangers in the helicopter revetments getting ready to load out on a UH-1 Huey for a mission insertion. Each man has a full load of water, ammunition and smoke grenades. Two of the team are armed with CAR-15s while another carries a full size M-16A-1. (U.S. Army, Fort Campbell Museum)

Team members jump from the insertion helicopter as the back up UH-1 passes overhead. This was the most dangerous time for a team, when they were in the open and the helicopter was in a hover close to the ground. If the helicopters came under fire they would have to back off until the escorting gunships could silence the guns. (U.S. Army)

A LRRP team from the 75th Rangers moves into a wood line after being inserted. The point man is alreadyout of signt in the brush. The team was being monitored by the back up Huey until it was safely under cover. (U.S. Army)

This LRRP team member is using a regular Army issue ruck sack frame to carry his gear. Most men preferred to cut the frame down so they could get more items on the pistol belt and so the back of the frame would hit them higher up on their back. The ruck sacks that we got from the 5th Special Forces group allowed us to carry our equipment better. (U.S. Army)

A team radioman from Company L, 75th Rangers (LRRP), which replaced Company F, 58th Infantry (LRRP) in the101st Airborne after February of 1969. The long antenna for the radio can be seen stuck down in his rucksack. The total weight pf the ruck sack was some thirty-eight pounds. (U. S Army, Fort Campbell Museum)

After securing the extraction LZ the team took a minute to pose for a group photo. The man on the far left is a combat photographer with the 101st Airborne PIO office. The men are still using the lemon shaped hand grenade that can be seen on the front ammo pouches of Harris and Brooks. Three of the men have cloth ammunition bandoleers draped across their chests with each of the seven pockets loaded with a full M-16 magazine. This allowed us to carry more rounds and kept them within reach. (U. S. Army)

SP\4 Taylor examines two 82MM mortar rounds found by the team while checking out a enemy camp during a patrol in the I Corp area. The team also uncovered some 57MM recoiless rifle rounds. The ammo was dropped into a creek near the site since we could not destroy it without making noise which would give us away. (U.S. Army)

Combat Troops Of World War II
From
squadron/signal publications

3003

3008

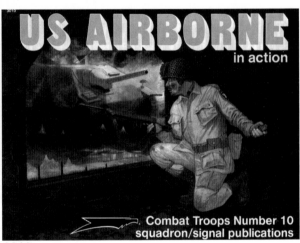

3010

squadron/signal publications